P9-CMX-771

WITHDRAWN

Learning to Write Narrative Paragraphs

Frances Purslow

WEIGL PUBLISHERS INC.
Fitchburg Public Library
5530 Lacy Road
Fitchburg, WI 53711

Published by Weigl Publishers Inc.
350 5th Avenue, Suite 3304, PMB 6G
New York, NY 10118-0069

Website: www.weigl.com
Copyright ©2008 WEIGL PUBLISHERS INC.
All rights reserved. No part of this publication may be reproduced, stored in a retrieval system, or transmitted in any form or by any means, electronic, mechanical, photocopying, recording, or otherwise, without the prior written permission of the publisher.

All of the Internet URLs given in the book were valid at the time of publication. However, due to the dynamic nature of the Internet, some addresses may have changed, or sites may have ceased to exist since publication. While the author and publisher regret any inconvenience this may cause readers, no responsibility for any such changes can be accepted by either the author or the publisher.

Library of Congress Cataloging-in-Publication Data

Purslow, Frances.
Narrative paragraphs / Frances Purslow.
p. cm. -- (Learning to write)
Includes index.
ISBN 978-1-59036-733-9 (hard cover : alk. paper) -- ISBN 978-1-59036-734-6 (soft cover : alk. paper)
1. Composition (Language arts)--Juvenile literature. 2. English language--Paragraphs--Juvenile literature.
3. Narration (Rhetoric)--Juvenile literature. I. Title.
LB1576.P8754 2008
372.62'3--dc22
2007012718

Printed in the United States of America
1 2 3 4 5 6 7 8 9 0 11 10 09 08 07

Editor: Heather C. Hudak
Design: Terry Paulhus

Every reasonable effort has been made to trace ownership and to obtain permission to reprint copyright material. The publishers would be pleased to have any errors or omissions brought to their attention so that they may be corrected in subsequent printings.

Table of Contents

4 Learning about Narrative Paragraphs

6 What Are Verbs?

8 Finding Transitions

10 Parts of a Narrative Paragraph

12 Creating a Timeline

14 Understanding Unity

16 Creating Coherence

18 Tools for Paragraph Writing

20 Put Your Knowledge to Use

22 Types of Paragraphs

23 Websites for Further Research

24 Glossary/Index

Learning about Narrative Paragraphs

A narrative paragraph is a group of sentences that tells what happens, how the action happens, and in what order the events occur. Authors use narrative paragraphs to share a story with readers. A narrative paragraph may be complete by itself, or it may be part of a longer piece of writing.

The following is an example of a narrative paragraph. It tells about an imaginary event in the life of a famous **frontiersman** named Davy Crockett.

Davy was born in Tennessee in 1786. People told wild stories about his strength and skills. One day when Davy Crockett was only 3 years old, a bear wandered into the cabin where he lived. When the bear began to eat some of Davy's favorite jam, the young boy grabbed the animal in a bear hug. He squeezed him until the bear finally dropped the jam and ran away.

Davy was elected to the government. He worked for the Tennessee **legislature**. Later, he was elected to Congress.

For a timeline of events in Davy's life, go to **www.infoporium.com/heritage/crockbio.shtml**. Use the timeline to write a story about Davy Crockett. Does his appearance give you some clues to what his life might have been like?

Follow the Action

Some legends are written about real people, such as Davy Crockett. Others are told about imaginary folk heroes, such as Paul Bunyan, a giant **lumberjack**. In the 1800s, loggers made up stories about this very large, strong man. The following narrative paragraph tells a story about Paul Bunyan as a baby. While reading, follow the action in the story. Look for the words that tell the action.

Paul Bunyan weighed between 80 and 100 pounds when he was born. At 3 weeks of age, he rolled over in his sleep and flattened 4 miles of forest. After that, Paul's parents made him a wooden cradle to sleep in. Then, they placed the cradle in the town's harbor so the waves could rock Paul to sleep. While floating in his cradle, the giant baby began to rock from side to side. This action caused large waves to form. The waves flooded small towns along the coast.

Look at the sketch of Paul Bunyan. Write two sentences about an action that this large man might have taken. Then circle the action word in each of your sentences.

What Are Verbs?

A narrative paragraph requires many action words. Action words are called verbs. A writer uses action words to tell what happened in a story.

The following narrative paragraph tells about the life of John Chapman. For 50 years, John traveled across the United States planting apple trees. These trees provided food for early settlers. Over time, he became known as Johnny Appleseed. Look for the verbs in the paragraph.

As a young boy, Johnny Appleseed loved nature. The wild animals in the woods became his friends. At 23 years of age, he left home. Johnny wanted to see the rich farmland out west. He walked for hundreds of miles. Johnny traveled light. He carried only some food in a bag.

From the painting of Johnny Appleseed, you can see that he did not care about money. However, he did care about apple trees. He gave apple trees to many poor settlers in the West. Go to **www.americanfolklore.net**. Click on "Heroes and Villains" to find more information about Johnny Appleseed. Make a list of verbs describing Johnny's actions.

Learning to Use Strong Verbs

The following narrative paragraph tells about another U.S. folk hero.

Phoebe Anne Mosey was born in 1860. Most people know her as Annie Oakley. She adopted this name when she performed as a sharpshooter. As a young girl, Annie taught herself how to use a gun so she could hunt for food. She competed in shooting contests. As an expert ***markswoman*** *and horseback rider, Annie won many medals and other awards. She could hit almost any target. Later, she entertained audiences in Buffalo Bill's Wild West Show.*

What actions did Annie Oakley perform in the paragraph? She was born. Then, she adopted, performed, taught, hunted, competed, won, hit, and entertained. These actions are verbs. They are strong verbs that help paint a picture of this independent woman.

What do you learn from the photo of Annie Oakley? Visit **www.pbs.org/wgbh/amex/oakley/index.html** to learn more about Annie. Write a few sentences about her life. Be sure to use strong verbs that tell the reader what she was like. Then, read the following sentence.

Annie Oakley rode around the show ring on her horse.

Now replace "rode" with a stronger verb. Use a thesaurus to find alternate words for "rode." You might replace it with "galloped," "raced," or "cantered." What other words can you find?

Finding Transitions

Connecting words, such as "then," "next," and "finally," help show the order of time. These connecting words are called transitions. They connect sentences and show the sequence of events.

The following paragraph tells about early explorers Lewis and Clark. Notice the transitions that show the order of time.

In 1803, the United States paid about $15 million to France for the Louisiana Territory. The Louisiana Purchase doubled the size of the United States. A year later, President Thomas Jefferson sent Meriwether Lewis and William Clark to explore and map the new territory. Then, when they returned, Lewis and Clark reported that there were many plants, fur-bearing animals, such as beavers, and American Indians living in the Pacific northwest. Later, more explorers traveled the area in search of furs.

Using Transitions

Look at the route marked on the map. This route, plus the transitions in the sentences below, will help you figure out the correct order of the sentences.

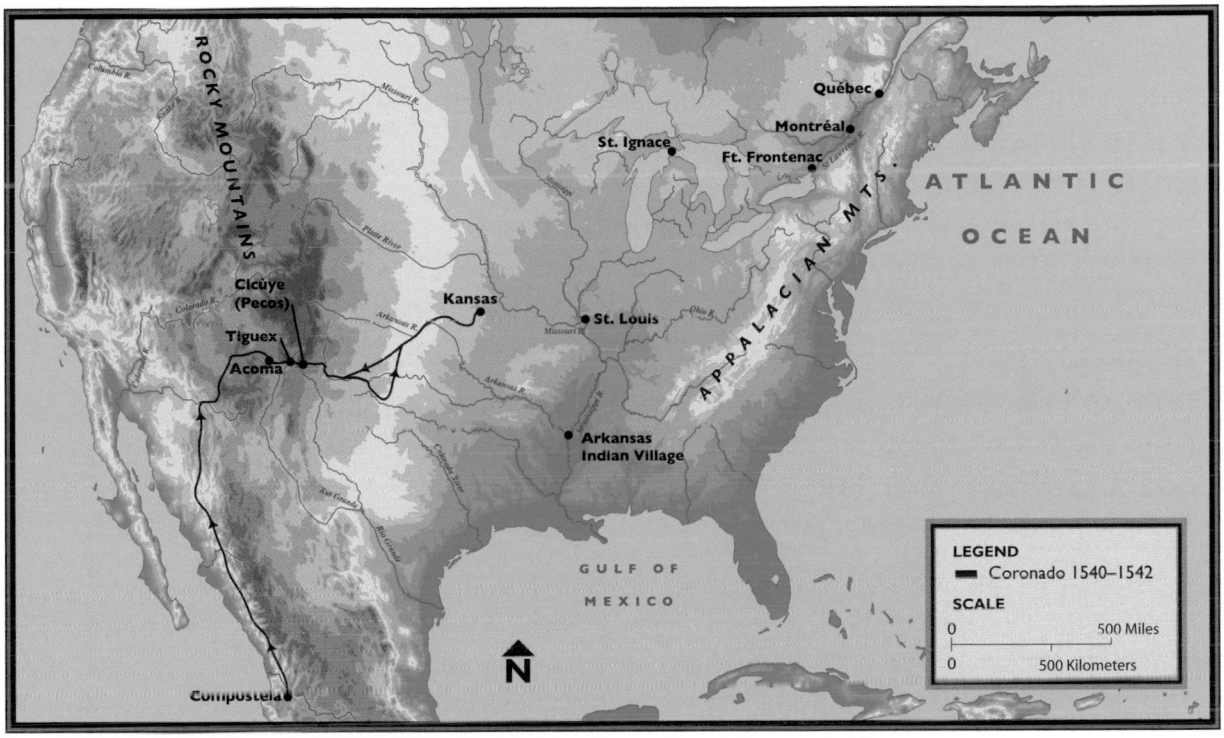

A. In 1540, Spanish explorer Francisco Vasquez de Coronado became the first European to explore southwestern North America. He was searching for gold in the legendary Seven Cities of Cibola.

B. Finally, he returned home without any of the riches he sought. However, his notes from his travels provided a detailed description of the southwestern United States.

C. Later, he traveled north to search for the wealthy kingdom of Quivira.

D. First, Coronado traveled from Mexico to the area now known as Arizona.

E. The next year, Coronado traveled east through New Mexico and Texas. There, he saw bison for the first time.

Answers: 1. A 2. D 3. E 4. C 5. B

Parts of a Narrative Paragraph

A narrative paragraph has three parts. The first part is the topic sentence. The topic sentence is usually the first sentence. It tells readers what the paragraph is about and catches their attention. For example, the topic sentence in the paragraph below introduces **civil rights activist**, Rosa Parks.

The supporting sentences generally follow the topic sentence. They provide details explaining or supporting the topic sentence. The events of the story being told unfold in the supporting sentences. They describe the events that led to Rosa's actions against **racism**.

At the end of a narrative paragraph, a sentence is needed to wrap up, or summarize, the ideas expressed in the paragraph. It brings the paragraph to a close and satisfies the readers' expectations. This is called the concluding sentence. It is usually a strong statement.

Rosa Parks was a remarkable woman. She was born in Alabama in 1913. When Rosa was growing up, most public places in the southern United States were ***segregated****. There were separate places for African Americans to sit on buses and trains, theaters, churches, and parks. Rosa's grandparents taught her to stand up for her rights. One day in 1955, Rosa was told by a bus driver that she would have to give up her seat for a passenger of European ancestry. Rosa refused, even though she knew she would be arrested. That day, Rosa stood up for her rights by staying seated.*

The topic sentence is shown in red in the paragraph. Can you tell which are the supporting and concluding sentences?

EXERCISE

Identifying the Parts

Dr. Martin Luther King, Jr., believed people should stand up for their civil rights. He believed that everyone deserved fair and equal treatment. He gave powerful speeches that brought hope to people all over the world. Dr. King supported Rosa Parks in her bus ***boycott****. He encouraged other African Americans in the United States to stay off the buses until the law was changed.*

For more information about this great man, go to **www.thekingcenter.org**. Write a topic sentence about Dr. Martin Luther King, Jr. Then write two or three supporting sentences telling some events in his life. Finally, write a strong, concluding sentence.

Creating a Timeline

Before writing a narrative paragraph, it helps to organize the events you are going to include. A timeline will help you do this. The events can be shown in the correct order on the organizer. For example, this timeline outlines key events in the life of Helen Keller. Helen became visually and hearing impaired when she was very young. She grew up to become a famous author and presenter. She used her fame to help others.

June 27, 1880 Helen Keller is born in Tuscumbia, Alabama. When she is 19 months old, Helen has a severe illness that causes her to become seeing and hearing impaired.

1887 Anne Sullivan becomes Helen's teacher. Anne teaches Helen how to communicate. Over time, Helen learns to speak, read **braille**, and write.

1900 Helen is accepted to Radcliffe College. She graduates in 1904.

1902 Helen publishes her first book, called *The Story of My Life*.

1915 Helen founds Helen Keller International, a non-profit organization that helps make life better for seeing **impaired** people all over the world. She begins to travel to give lectures about ways to prevent visual impairment.

1964 Helen is awarded the Presidential Medal of Freedom for her contribution to society.

Think about the events in your life. The timeline of your life would include things that have happened from your birth to the present. Use photos and key events to make a timeline of your life.

EXERCISE

Making the Sentences Flow

Amelia Earhart was an American aviator, or pilot. In 1928, she became the first female pilot to fly across the Atlantic Ocean alone. Amelia was also the first woman to receive the Distinguished Flying Cross. In June 1937, Amelia and ***navigator*** *Frank Noonan began a flight around the world. Their plane disappeared during the flight, and they were never found.*

Look at the pictures of Amelia Earhart on this page. Each picture is from a different time in Amelia's life. Use the information at **www.ameliaearhart.com** to write a timeline of the events in these photos. Be sure to include other key events in her life.

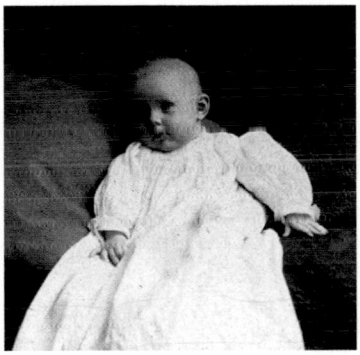

Understanding Unity

All of the sentences in a narrative paragraph should relate to the same topic. This is called unity. If a paragraph does not have unity, then one or more sentences do not relate to the main idea.

The following paragraph has unity. All of the sentences are about the voyages of Christopher Columbus.

The king and queen of Spain sent Italian explorer Christopher Columbus to look for a new route from Europe to Asia. Instead of a route to Asia, Columbus and his crew reached the Americas on October 12, 1492. Later, Columbus made three more voyages to the Americas. He explored the areas around Cuba, Jamaica, and the Canary Islands. Columbus never explored the land that became the United States.

EXERCISE

Which Sentence Does Not Belong?

The following paragraph does not have unity. It includes a sentence that does not relate to the main topic. Find the sentence that is out of place in this narrative paragraph.

Columbus had promised the Spanish king and queen that he would find a route to Asia. He died believing that the Caribbean Islands he visited were part of Asia. Spanish explorer Juan Ponce de León was the first European to visit Florida. Columbus did not realize that he had actually reached the Americas.

Look at the drawing of Columbus' three ships, the *Nina*, the *Pinta*, and the *Santa Maria,* as they set sail from Spain. Imagine an adventure aboard one of them. Write a narrative paragraph about such an adventure. Make sure that all of the sentences in your paragraph relate to your topic.

Creating Coherence

The ideas in a paragraph should flow in a logical order from beginning to end. This is called coherence. Transitions can be used to create coherence in a paragraph.

The following paragraph is about an Powhatan girl named Pocahontas. Pocahontas was born in Virginia in 1595. She was the daughter of a powerful chief. The following paragraph tells how Pocahontas helped European settlers. Notice the transitions that show the order of time.

Pocahontas was 12 years old when she first met British settlers. These settlers traveled to Virginia to make their homes. As a result, a community was built near Pocahontas' village. This community was called Jamestown. Often, Pocahontas would visit Jamestown to help the settlers. She would bring food to keep them from dying of starvation. Today, Pocahontas is remembered for showing great kindness to the settlers. According to legend, Captain Smith said Pocahontas' father planned to kill him. However, Pocahontas stopped her father and saved Captain Smith's life. Many experts believe Captain's Smith's story is false. They believe the Powhatans were holding a welcoming ritual for Captain Smith.

Research other folk heroes, such as Casey Jones and Doc Holliday, and write a coherent paragraph about an event in that person's life.

EXERCISE

Put These Sentences in Order

The following sentences explain how astronaut Neil Armstrong became the first person to walk on the Moon. Can you figure out the correct order of the sentences to create a narrative paragraph with coherence? Look for clues to the correct order.

A. Four days later, Aldrin and Armstrong climbed into the landing craft called the *Eagle* to complete their trip to the Moon.

B. Then, Armstrong and Aldrin returned to their spacecraft and headed back to Earth.

C. As they touched down on the Moon, they were surprised by the huge boulders on its surface.

D. For more than two hours, they collected samples, set up instruments, and planted the U.S. flag.

E. On July 16, 1969, Michael Collins, Neil Armstrong, and Edwin "Buzz" Aldrin, Jr., boarded the *Apollo 11*.

F. Armstrong stepped out first onto the powdery surface of the Moon.

G. Nineteen minutes later, Aldrin joined him.

H. On July 24, they safely splashed into the Pacific Ocean off the coast of Hawai'i.

Answers: 1. E 2. A 3. C 4. F 5. G 6. D 7. B 8. H

Tools for Paragraph Writing

What did you learn? Look at the questions in the "Skills" column. Compare them to the page number in the "Page" column. Refresh your memory about the content you learned during this part of the paragraph writing process by reading the "Content" column below.

SKILLS	CONTENT	PAGE
What is a narrative paragraph?	Davy Crockett, Paul Bunyan	4–5
What are verbs?	 Johnny Appleseed, Annie Oakley	6–7
How are transitions useful?	Lewis & Clark, Francisco Vasquez de Coronado	8–9
What are the parts of a narrative paragraph?	 Rosa Parks, Dr. Martin Luther King, Jr.	10–11
How is a timeline useful?	Helen Keller, Amelia Earhart	12–13
What is unity?	 Christopher Columbus	14–15
What is coherence?	Pocahontas, Neil Armstrong, Buzz Aldrin, Michael Collins	16–17

Practice Writing Different Types of Sentences

Look at the photograph. It shows the heroes who risked their lives to save others after terrorists attacked the World Trade Center in September 2001.

On September 11, 2001, Americans were shocked by ***terrorist*** *attacks that took place in their country. Terrorists hijacked planes and drove them into New York's World Trade Center, the Pentagon in Virginia, and a field in Pennsylvania. Firefighters and rescue workers were true heroes as they struggled to save lives. It was a terrible day! Americans bonded in their plight to overcome the attacks. How did they react?*

Use the Internet, or visit the library to find out more information about the heroes of September 11, 2001. Then, write four narrative sentences about the events in the picture. Try writing one of each of the following types of sentences.

In a telling sentence, the writer tells about something. This sentence ends with a period.

Asking sentences ask questions. They end with a question mark.

An exclaiming sentence shows emotion. It ends with an exclamation point.

Commanding sentences give direct orders. They end with a period.

Put Your Knowledge to Use

Put your knowledge of narrative paragraphs to use by writing about a person you consider a hero. The hero could be someone you know, someone famous, or someone you created out of your imagination. Remember that a narrative paragraph tells a story.

Here is a photograph of Mohandas Gandhi. The paragraph about Gandhi has a topic sentence, supporting sentences, and a concluding sentence. The sentences flow in a logical order and are related to each other. There are many verbs throughout the text.

While the world was at war, Mohandas Gandhi was protesting against violence. He achieved his aims by inspiring people to take part in nonviolent protests. All of his victories were achieved without bloodshed. For 20 years, Gandhi had worked for the rights of Indians in South Africa. He returned home to India during World War I to press for independence from Great Britain. He became a symbol of independent India and was called Mahatma, meaning "great soul." After years of battling for his people and being jailed for his efforts, Gandhi saw India become independent in 1947.

Choose one of the three people pictured below to research. Before you begin to write your paragraph, make a timeline of the events. Begin with the event that happened first. Then add the events that followed. End with the last event.

As you write your narrative paragraph, make sure that it has a topic sentence, supporting sentences, and a concluding sentence. Choose only sentences that relate to your topic. Finally, be sure that the ideas in your paragraph flow in a logical order from beginning to end. After writing your paragraph, identify the verbs you used. Can you replace some of the verbs with stronger ones?

Steve Irwin

Condoleezza Rice

David Beckham

EXPANDED CHECKLIST

Reread your paragraph, and make sure that you have all of the following.

- ☑ My paragraph has a topic sentence.
- ☑ My paragraph has supporting sentences.
- ☑ My paragraph has a concluding sentence.
- ☑ All of the sentences in my paragraph relate to the same topic.
- ☑ All of the ideas in my paragraph flow in a logical order.
- ☑ My paragraph has strong verbs.

Types of Paragraphs

Now, you have learned the tools for writing narrative paragraphs. You can use your knowledge of verbs, transitions, timelines, parts of a paragraph, unity, and coherence to write narrative paragraphs. There are three other types of paragraphs. You can use some of the same tools you learned in this book to write all types of paragraphs. The chart below shows other types of paragraphs and their key features.

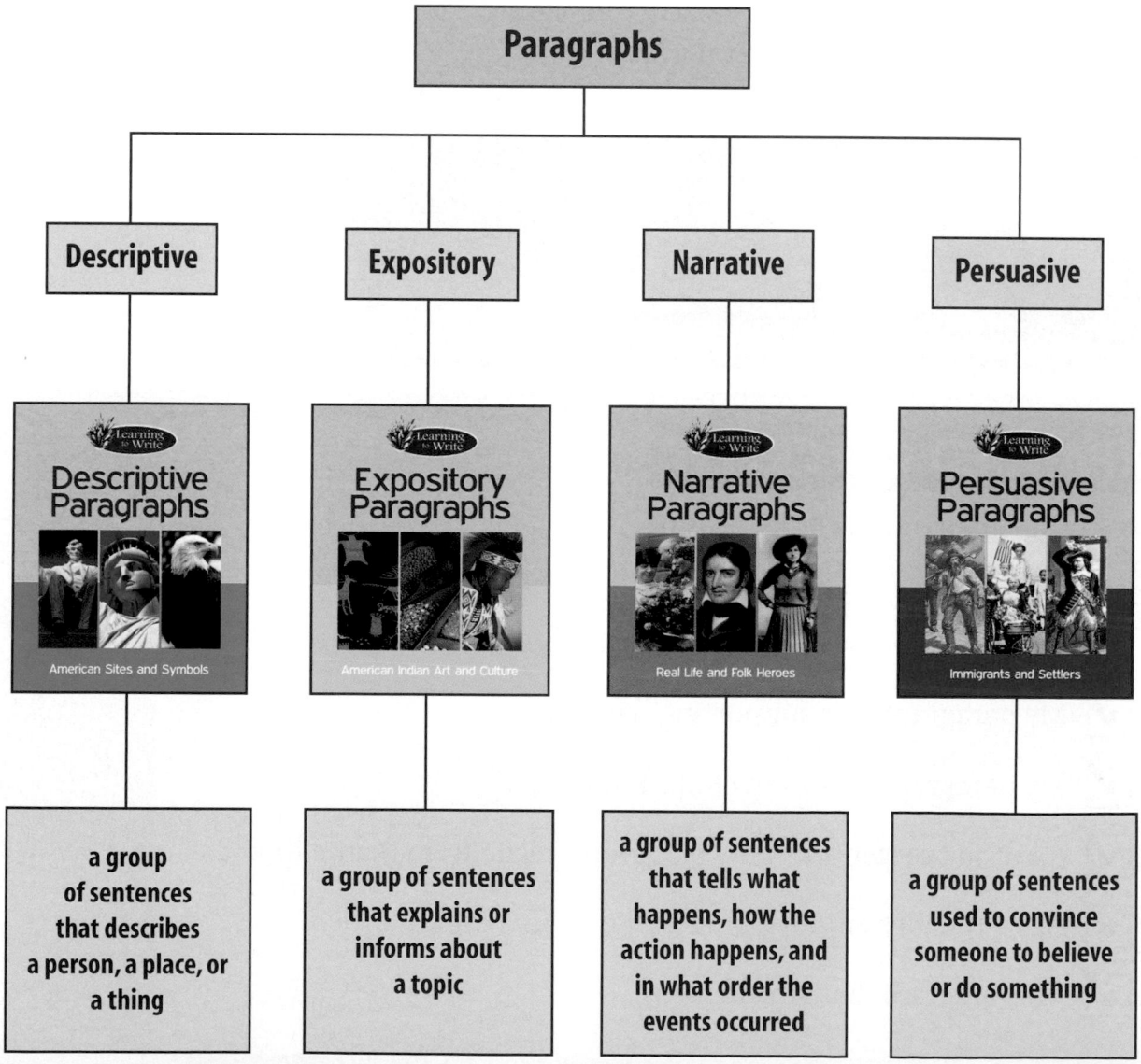

Websites for Further Research

Many books and websites provide information on writing narrative paragraphs. To learn more about writing this type of paragraph, borrow books from the library, or surf the Internet.

To find out more about writing narrative paragraphs, type key words, such as "writing paragraphs," into the search field of your Web browser. There are many sites that teach about heroes. You can use these sites to practice writing narrative paragraphs. Begin by selecting one topic from the site. Read about the topic, and then use the checklist on page 21 to write a paragraph.

Visit *Sporting Heroes* to learn about athletes from around the world who have made great strides in their sport.
www.sporting-heroes.net

My Hero provides a directory and brief biography of many people who have achieved success in different areas of interest, such as science, sports, and writers.
www.myhero.com

Glossary

activist: a person who is engaged in political activity

boycott: to refuse to use a product or service in order to change the way that product or service is delivered

braille: a type of written language that is used by the seeing impaired; raised dots that represent letters and numbers

civil rights: the right to have political freedom and equality

frontiersman: a person living in a region that is between settled and unsettled country

impaired: weakened or damaged

legislature: government of a place

lumberjack: a person who cuts down trees and transports them to a mill

markswoman: a woman who is skilled at shooting

navigator: a person who guides the route of a vehicle

racism: dislike of a person because of his or her culture

segregated: to have public places that are separated for people of different cultures

terrorist: a person who uses violence to achieve his or goals

Index

Aldrin, Buzz 17, 18
Appleseed, Johnny 6, 18
Armstrong, Neil 17, 18

Bunyan, Paul 5, 18

Clark, William 8, 18
coherence 16, 17, 18, 22
Columbus, Christopher 14, 15, 18
concluding sentence 10, 11, 20, 21
Crockett, Davy 4, 5, 18

Earhart, Amelia 13, 18

Keller, Helen 12, 18
King, Martin Luther, Jr. 11, 18

Lewis, Meriwether 8, 18

Oakley, Annie 7, 18

Parks, Rosa 10, 11, 18
Pocahontas 16, 18

supporting sentences 10, 11, 20, 21

topic sentence 10, 11, 20, 21
transitions 8, 9, 16, 18, 22

unity 14, 15, 18, 22

verbs 6, 7, 18, 20, 21, 22